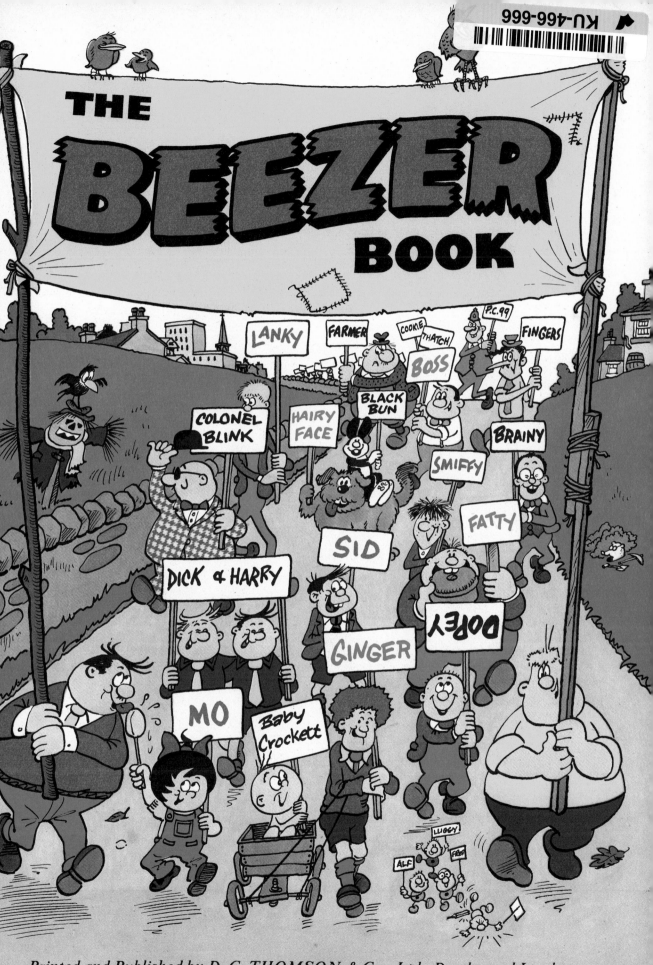

Printed and Published by D. C. THOMSON & Co., Ltd., Dundee and London.

"GO FOR YOUR GUN!" STARTS THE FUN.

LATER.

COO! I'M THIRSTY TODAY!

SPLOSH!

HAVE A DRINK, POP!

YOU STUPID CLOTS! NOW LOOK WHAT YOU'VE DONE WITH YOUR FOOLING ABOUT! YOU'VE KNOCKED MUM'S PLANT DOWN!

HERE, HANG IT UP AGAIN! AND LET'S HAVE NO MORE TRICKS!

ER—HOW ABOUT HANGING IT UP HERE, POP? IT WOULD BE FARTHER FROM THE DOOR!

YES, THAT'LL DO!

YES, THAT'S THE SPOT, DICK!

HO-HO!

IT SURE IS—SMACK ON THE WATER PIPE!

SPLOSH!

BULL'S-EYE!

OKAY! I KNOW WHEN I'M BEATEN! LET'S GO TO THE CIRCUS!

YIPPEE!

AW, CHEER UP, POP! ENJOY THE SHOW!

GRR! I HATE CIRCUSES!

SPLOSH!

HA-HA! WHAT A LAUGH! YOU WERE GREAT, JUMBO! OH-HO-HO! WONDERFUL! MORE! MORE!

BAH!

Baby Crockett

WATCH *the*

TAWNY OWL

MAGPIE

GOLDCREST

NUTHATCH

LONG-TAILED TIT

TAWNY OWL

MAGPIE

NUTHATCH

GOLDCREST

BIRDIE!

JAY

GREAT SPOTTED
WOODPECKER

BLACKCAP

LONG-TAILED TIT

BLACKCAP

GREAT SPOTTED WOODPECKER

JAY

The IRON EATERS

THE sea was calm and gulls were wheeling overhead as the giant oil tanker steamed up the English Channel. Everything seemed peaceful. But, unknown to the crew, deadly danger was lurking nearby. Bobbing about in the sea was a small pink sponge. It looked harmless—but that tiny sponge was capable of sinking the tanker!

SCOTTISH PRINCE

s an Iron Eater—a strange creature from which ate iron. As the tanker passed nearby the sponge veered towards it.

It soon caught up with the tanker and leaped hungrily on to the rudder.

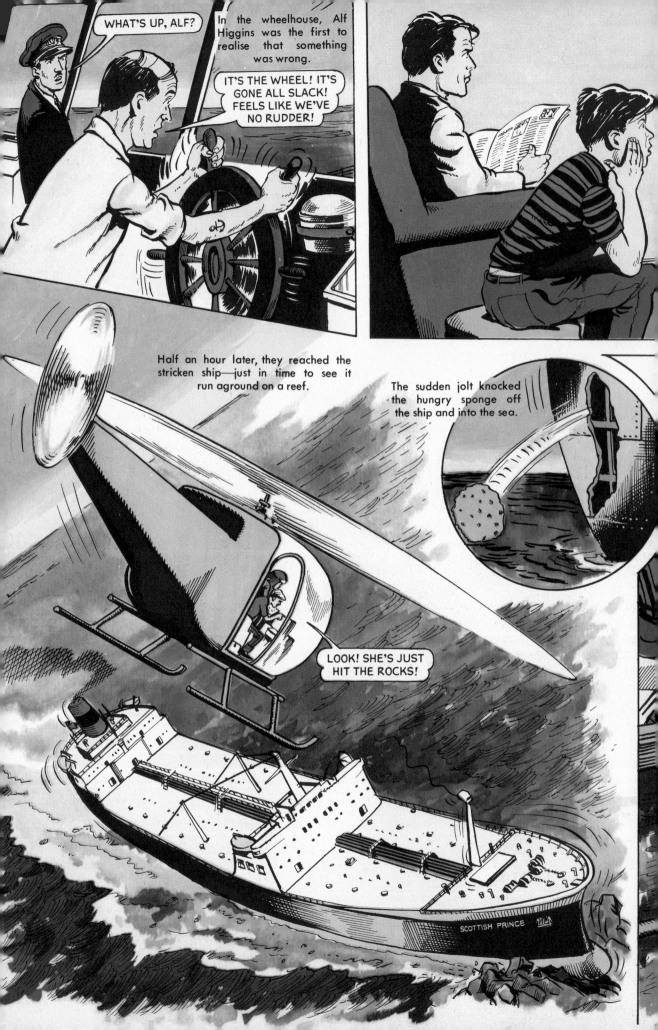

It wasn't long before the news of the stricken tanker was being flashed on the television screens. At once, young Tommy Robertson and his father sprang into action.

...NDS LIKE THE ...K OF THE IRON ...RS, DAD. WE'D ...ER GET OUT ...E AND SEE IF ...CAN HELP.

THE TANKER "SCOTTISH PRINCE" IS DRIFTING OUT OF CONTROL IN THE ENGLISH CHANNEL AFTER MYSTERIOUSLY LOSING HER RUDDER.

Professor Robertson was leading the fight against the Iron Eaters and there was a helicopter parked outside ready for such an emergency.

START HER UP, JIM. THERE'S TROUBLE IN THE CHANNEL!

Pluckily, Tommy volunteered to climb down and catch the sponge.

CAREFUL, SON!

I'LL LIFT IT OUT OF THE WATER BEFORE IT GOES BACK TO THE TANKER!

THERE'S THE TROUBLE! IT'S AN IRON EATER ALL RIGHT!

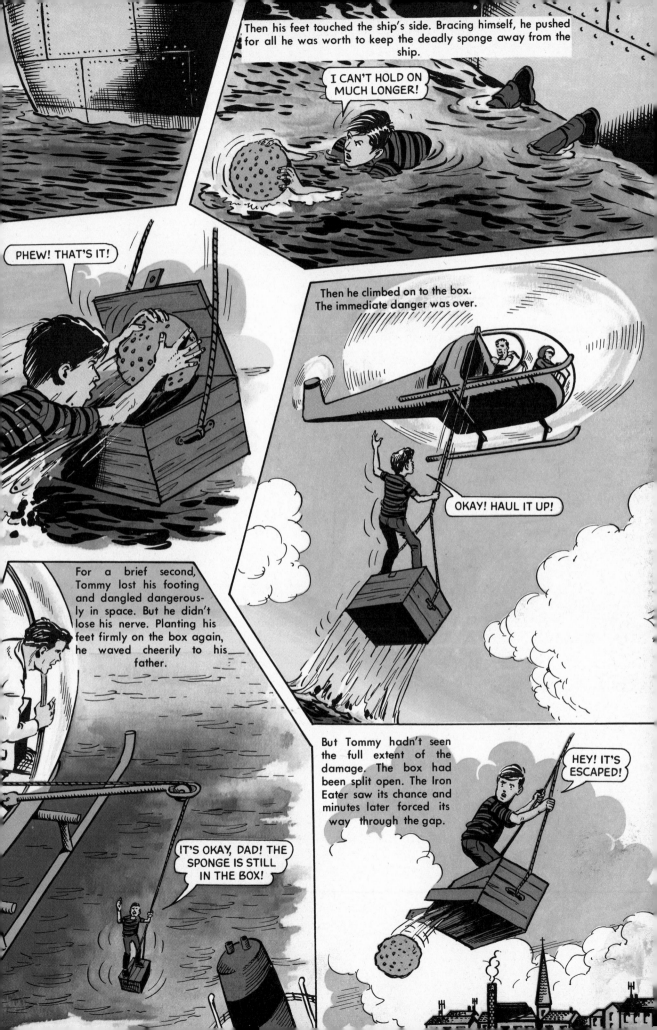

Meanwhile, the helicopter was coming down fast, but even before it reached the beach, Tommy leapt off and sprinted towards the youngsters.

DON'T TOUCH THAT! IT'S DANGEROUS!

WHAT'S HE SHOUTING ABOUT—IT'S ONLY A BALL?

KICK IT OVER HERE!

...nd every one headed back out to sea towards the ...anker. Tommy gaped in horror. If they reached the ...hip it would soon be riddled like a sieve, and its ...argo of oil would ruin the beaches for miles around.

THEY'RE FUNNY FISHES, MUM.

Tommy raced up the beach—

...Y! ...THEM ...E!

— then sprinted outside.

YOU CAN'T DO THAT! STOP!

GSB 836F

YOUNG SID
THE COPPER'S KID

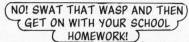

THE BANANA BUNCH

NUMSKULLS

THINK I'LL DO MY ACCOUNTS BOOK.

CLICK! CLICK!

BRAIN DEPT.

OH, NO! THAT MEANS LOTS OF BRAIN WORK FOR ME! GRR!

I'M JUST NOT DOING IT!

FORGET ACCOUNTS. GO FOR A WALK.

SUGGESTION BOX

SOON.

UP THE TUFF ST GANG

LET'S CHASE HIM OUT OF OUR DISTRICT, GANG.

OOER! TOUGH LITTLE URCHINS!

YAH!

YAH!

YAH!

BETTER GET OUR MAN HOME, BRAINY! SOME URCHINS ARE TRYING TO BRAIN HIM WITH HALF-BRICKS.

IF THOSE URCHINS INJURE HIM, HE'LL HAVE TO STAY IN THE HOUSE AND SURE AS FATE HE'LL START DOING HIS ACCOUNTS TO PASS THE TIME.

HEH-HEH! IT'S NOT HOLIDAY TIME SO THERE'LL BE NO URCHINS TO DO HIM ANY HARM.

HOP ON A TRAIN TO THE SEA-SIDE.

SUGGESTION BOX

AND SO.

PLEASANT HERE WITH NO URCHINS TO BOTHER ME.

WAH! I'VE STOOD ON A SEA URCHIN!

WELL, I CAN'T GO OUT WITH MY FOOT LIKE THIS, SO I MIGHT AS WELL GET MY ACCOUNTS DONE.

GRR! SOME DAYS YOU JUST CAN'T WIN!

ER

BEEZER

Someone has stolen the let[ters] of the word 'Beezer' from [the] notice board. Can you [help] P.C. 99 to find them hid[den] around the farm?

Dick has rounded up 26 sheep plus half the number that Harry has rounded up. How many sheep has Dick rounded up if there are 200 sheep on the farm?

The Badd Lads want to make a quick escape from Farmer. Which rope should they untie to free the horse?

Dicky Burd fancies a feed from these sacks, but Farmer has got the names mixed up. Can you sort them out so that your little pal knows what's in them?

TEEZERS

Can you spot the nine deliberate mistakes which our artist has made when drawing the house?

Join the dots in numerical order to find out why Ginger is running.

Colonel Blink thinks the hens he is feeding are all the same, but one is different. Can you spot it?

The pattern on the flowers changes as you look from left to right. Can you help Smiffy to find out what the fifth flower should look like?

ANSWERS:
Sheep puzzle—Dick has rounded up 84 sheep.
Deliberate mistakes—Light is upside-down. Dog's kennel on the roof. Break in TV aerial. Fireplace on end wall. Shed has no roof. Drain-pipe goes inside house. House number is upside-down. Door hinges and handle on the same side. Window box upside-down.
Different hens—The hen nearest Blink has one leg coloured yellow.
Rope puzzle—The Badd Lads will have to untie rope C.
Sack puzzle—The sacks contain cement, firewood, barley and wheat.
Missing letters—B is in the bushes behind Pop; E in the wall above Pop's head; E on the front of the tractor; Z in the trees above Dick; E in the brickwork on the front of the house and R is on the horse's stirrup.
Flower pattern—The flower should look like this:-

FUN, BY GOSH, IN THE HOTEL POSH!

THE HILLYS and THE BILLYS

GARDEN WARBLER

WATCH THE BIRDIE!

HOUSE MARTIN

CUCKOO

WHINCHAT

HOOPOE

SWALLOW

REDSTART

SWIFT

PIED
FLYCATCHER

NECHAT

SEDGE WARBLER

PIED FLYCATCHER

SEDGE WARBLER

GARDEN WARBLER

REDSTART

STONECHAT

WHINCHAT

SWALLOW

HOUSE MARTIN

SWIFT

CUCKOO

HOOPOE

BLACK BUN

HELLO, SQUIRE! FARMER HERE. IT'S A FINE DAY FOR A RABBIT SHOOT. MEET ME IN FIFTEEN MINUTES.

EH?

A RABBIT SHOOT! WHAT A CHEEK! I'LL SOON PUT A STOP TO THAT!

SO—

WONDER IF FARMER WILL LIKE THE LOOK OF THIS SNOWMAN?

KNOCK! KNOCK!

HE DOESN'T—

GRR! IF THAT'S SUPPOSED TO LOOK LIKE ME, IT DOESN'T!

I'LL KICK IT TO BITS— OOYAH!

OOOW! MY BRUISED TOOTSIES!

HA-HA! CLEVER ME—BUILT THE SNOWMAN OVER A TREE STUMP!

PRESENTLY—

HERE COMES THE SQUIRE. I'VE GOT A SURPRISE IN STORE FOR HIM.

FARMER! IT'S ME—SQUIRE LONGBEAK!

EEK!

ANOTHER UGLY SNOWMAN, EH?

WELL, I'LL SMASH IT TO BITS AGAIN!

I SUPPOSE YOU THOUGHT THAT WAS FUNNY, FARMER.

S-SQUIRE!

TAKE THAT!

OOYAH!

HO-HO! IT'S TURNED OUT TO BE A NICE FARMER SHOOT!

A SEAT AT THE FIRE? POP'S SURE A TRIER!

LITTLE MO

MY, OH, MY! A JUMPING PIE!

The Banana Bunch

HOWEVER, THERE ARE LOTS OF NIGHT-SHIFT WORKERS IN THE STREET!

BEAT IT, CATS!

MISSED!

OOF!

OUCH!

WELL, DOPEY'S DAFT IDEA'S DONE THE TRICK. WE'VE GOT LOTS OF JUMBLE NOW.

ON THE WAY TO THE JUMBLE SALE—

OH, NO! WE'VE GOT A PUNCTURE.

YOU STAND GUARD, FATTY, WHILE WE HAVE THE WHEEL REPAIRED.

AYE, AYE!

WE'LL FOOL FATTY WITH THIS PIE CRUST AND THEN GRAB THE JUMBLE.

SO—

MY! A PIE.

WOW! IT'S ALIVE!

COME HERE, PRETTY PIE!

HA-HA! WE PUT A FROG UNDER THAT PIE CRUST!

LET'S GO, MEN!

WE'LL LEAVE THE BOILER, IT'S TOO HEAVY.

Blaze
THE TALE OF A PLUCKY PONY

BLAZE was different from the other wild ponies in the New Forest. There were hundreds of them, browns and greys mostly, but Blaze was a piebald, with a white blaze on his forehead that gave him his name. He was always on the alert, always first to spot danger. That was why Blaze became the leader of a herd.

It was autumn, and Blaze and the herd were grazing in a clearing.

Suddenly, the peace of the forest was shattered as a truck roared out of the trees. The driver was a poacher, determined to round up the ponies.

At a flying gallop, Blaze led the ponies off through the forest.

Suddenly, just ahead he saw rows of poles and three men, shouting and waving their arms. It was a trap!

Once inside the corral there was no escape, and Blaze realised it. With an angry snort he charged at the two men holding the gate of the corral. Gate and poachers went down like ninepins.

Then Blaze headed off into the depths of the forest with the herd at his heels. The poachers gave up the chase, but they'd learned one thing—Blaze was no ordinary pony.

For the rest of the day all was quiet, but Blaze didn't relax. He kept a wary eye open for trouble. And it was just as well he did.

A foal was lying half asleep in the sun when out of a thicket sprang a fox. It reckoned the dozing foal was easy prey.

What it hadn't reckoned on was Blaze. The plucky pony exploded into action!

With a terrified yowl, the fox fled from the flashing teeth and flying hooves.

Far into the forest Blaze chased the fox, the[n] his way back to the herd he ran into more trou[ble.] The poachers' truck had roared into the cl[ear]ing separating him from the other ponies. "[...] keep that piebald moving," yelled Martin, [the] leader of the poachers. "Get him out of the [way] and we'll easily round up the others."

Poor Blaze didn't realise what the plan was. With the poachers right on his tail he had to flee.

Then, when Blaze was well away from the herd, the poachers swiftly headed back and got the rest of the ponies on the move.

And Martin was right. Without Blaze to lead them, the ponies were no match for the poachers. Within ten minutes they were all safely penned in the corral. Dick Martin was well pleased with himself. "Worth a few quid, that lot," he mused.

After the day's clear skies, night brought with it the first cold snap of the autumn, and Martin and his men were happy to be seated round the stove in their caravan. It was too bad one of them hadn't the sense to keep an eye on the herd—for Blaze was back! Eyes gleaming wickedly in the moonlight, he trotted towards the corral. CRASH! Wood splinters flew in all directions as the pony's powerful hindlegs smashed into the fencing.

Dick Martin had been foiled again. The rogue threw open his caravan door in time to see the ponies thundering away!

"It's that pesky piebald again!" snarled Martin. "Blast! We'll never catch up with them tonight! But I'll get you, Piebald! Just you wait!" Blaze, framed against the moon, snorted defiantly! Then he was gone!

Next morning found Blaze standing guard over the herd.

Then once again the poachers' blue truck came pitching and bouncing out of the bushes. Dick Martin knew now his only chance of rounding up the ponies was to catch Blaze first—and he was set on doing just that!

rly separating Blaze
the rest of the herd, they
e the pony into the trees.
ically Blaze dodged this
and that, but always the
was close behind. On
on ran Blaze till he
ed a main road. He sped
it, still at a headlong
gallop.

Houses loomed up, but still he kept going—right along the High Street of
Applecombe, and always the truck was there, drawing closer and closer.

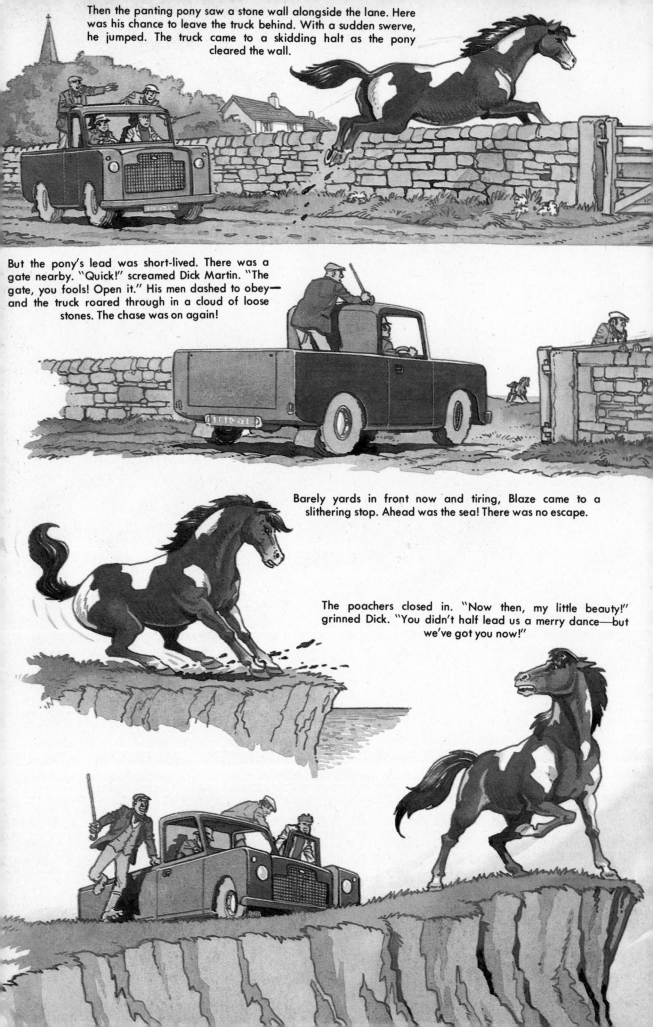

Then the panting pony saw a stone wall alongside the lane. Here was his chance to leave the truck behind. With a sudden swerve, he jumped. The truck came to a skidding halt as the pony cleared the wall.

But the pony's lead was short-lived. There was a gate nearby. "Quick!" screamed Dick Martin. "The gate, you fools! Open it." His men dashed to obey— and the truck roared through in a cloud of loose stones. The chase was on again!

Barely yards in front now and tiring, Blaze came to a slithering stop. Ahead was the sea! There was no escape.

The poachers closed in. "Now then, my little beauty!" grinned Dick. "You didn't half lead us a merry dance—but we've got you now!"

...aze hesitated only long enough to realise there ...as no other way out, then he jumped—clean over the ...f! The poachers were stunned. For a few seconds they ...od in disbelief, rooted to the spot, then they rushed forward.

...Looked to me like 'e meant that," gasped one. "Never ...ought it would come to that." "One thing's for sure ...—he's a goner now," said Dick. "Ain't seen anything like it before!"

...Martin was wrong. An hour later, on a sandy beach ...es away a piebald pony staggered ashore. Blaze ...d survived to fight another day. And fight he would.

CHIRPY'S FIRST FLIGHT ISN'T QUITE RIGHT!

DICKY BURD

I'VE NEVER FLOWN BEFORE, DICKY. WHAT'S IT LIKE?

AW! IT'S EASY, CHIRPY. JUST WATCH ME!

FIRST OF ALL YOU TAKE OFF LIKE THIS.

THEN FLAP YOUR WINGS UP AND DOWN. SEE?

DIP TO MAKE A TURN.

GLIDING IS REALLY EASY, CHIRPY!

CHIRPY! WHAT ON EARTH...?

THOUGHT I'D GET A LIFT TO START OFF, DICKY!

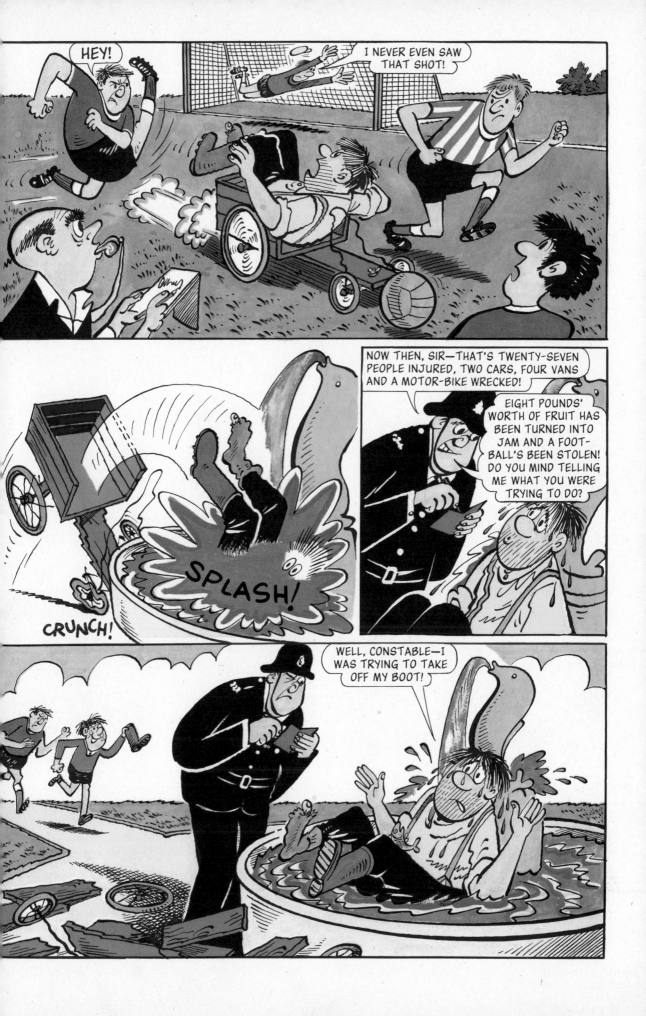

YOUNG SID

THE COPPER'S KID

OH, BOY! AUNT MABEL'S BOUGHT ME A POLICEMAN'S OUTFIT FOR MY BIRTHDAY!

KIDDY COP OUTFIT

I'LL TRY OUT THIS WHISTLE IN THE GARDEN AND SEE IF ANY COPS COME RUNNING!

PHEEP!

FIDO! YOU STUPID DOG! I WASN'T WHISTLING FOR YOU!

I KNOW! I'LL TRY OUT MY HANDCUFFS ON FIDO!

HO-HO! THEY WORK FINE!

THAT'LL KEEP FIDO OUT OF THE WAY WHILE I TRY OUT THE WHISTLE AGAIN.

THERE—I'VE NEARLY FINISHED POLISHING THE CAR!

PHEEP!

WATCH the

KITTIWAKE

GUILLEMOT

SHAG

FULMAR

FULMAR   KITTIWAKE   GUILLEMOT   SHAG

BIRDIE!

GANNET

BLACK GUILLEMOT

RAZORBILL

PUFFIN

RAZORBILL

PUFFIN

BLACK GUILLEMOT

GANNET

SO—

COLONEL BLINK

GOOD GRIEF! THIS CUPBOARD'S FILTHY!

THE OL' PLACE NEEDS SPRING CLEANING. I'LL GET THE CARPET BEATER...

...AND OFF TO WORK. ARF!

AHEM! WRONG HOUSE, BLINKY!

THERE'S NOTHING LIKE A SPOT OF WORK TO KEEP YOU IN TRIM! ARF! ARF!

I'LL MOVE ALL THE FURNITURE OUT INTO THE GARDEN FIRST!

OUR SHERIFF'S AN APE

SURE used to be some real rootin'-tootin' shootin' down Coyote Creek way, but not any more—no, siree—not since the Creek got its two sheriffs. Yeah, that's right—TWO! There's that young feller, Danny Blain, an' then there's his deputy, Charlie. Only Charlie ain't no ordinary deputy—he's a real, live ape! And nobody—except Charlie himself, of course—gets up to monkey tricks when he's around. Luke Lafferty was about to find that out...!

Charlie was polishin' off his eighth banana of the mornin' when Danny came out of the sheriff's office.

HEY, CHARLIE—THESE 'WANTED' POSTERS FOR LUKE LAFFERTY JUST CAME IN ON THAT STAGE. SPREAD 'EM OVER THE TOWN. SEEMS LAFFERTY HELD UP THE BANK OVER AT PINE CITY AND WAS LAST SEEN HEADING THIS WAY!

WANTED

$1000...

Charlie took the 'wanted' notices and ambled away across the main street.

SAM SMART'S GENERAL STORE

Sam Smart had a big boxful of nails on display outside his general store, and Charlie helped himself to one. He didn't need a hammer—not with that mighty mitt!

WHAM! Charlie biffed that there nail so hard he smashed the upright clean in two!

CRUNCH!

Too late, Sam took to his heels. Down came the roofin', tin tubs an' all!

GLUG!

When Sam pulled himself outa that barrel he was black with treacle—and red with rage!

YOU GREAT HAIRY GALOOT! GIT OUT O' HERE!

Charlie hung his head in shame and slunk away. But he soon cheered up when he came to a deserted shack on the outskirts o' the town. There was no one here to bawl him out.

Leastways, that's what he thought—but that shack wasn't as empty as it looked. Inside, a bearded gent was admirin' his reflection in a mirror.

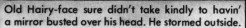

Outside, Charlie drew back his mitt to hammer up another notice. Suddenly—KER-RASH! The big ape had done it again!

Old Hairy-face sure didn't take kindly to havin' a mirror busted over his head. He stormed outside.

WHAT'S THE BIG IDEA?

By way of an apology, Charlie removed the offending mirror—what was left of it, that was. And then—surprise, surprise—Hairy-face's beard got caught in a jagged piece of glass, and off it came, too!

Difficult to say who was most surprised—Charlie or his victim. For who should the beardless boyo be but—yep—you've guessed it—Luke Lafferty himself!

WANTED
$1000.

Luke didn't hang around to admire his likeness. Away he went, just as fast as those bow legs o' his could carry him.

Luckily for Luke, young Hank Jones had just led a couple o' nags from the stable across to the drinking trough. Luke vaulted on to the back of one and stormed away.

HEY! YOU CAN'T TAKE THAT HOSS!

Charlie was close behind. And anything Luke could do, he could do, too—well, maybe . . .!

Charlie's vault would have been perfect, if only his nag hadn't chosen that moment to bend its neck to drink. SPLASH! Poor old Charlie dived head-first into that there trough!

Charlie came up spoutin' water like a whale. Shakin' his mitt at the fast-disappearin' crook, he clambered out o' the trough and hurried back to the sheriff's office.

GIT OUTA THAT WATER! IT'S FOR DRINKIN', NOT BATHIN'!

Two ticks later, he was doin' his best to get the message over to young Danny.

WHASSAT? LAFFERTY HERE IN TOWN? WHEN? WHERE?

WANTE

$1000.

The angry ape led Danny to the old shack.

IN THERE? GOSH, HE MUST HAVE BEEN USIN' IT AS A HIDE-OUT!

WE'D BETTER HAVE A LOOK AROUND! COO! IT'S DARK IN HERE!

OKAY. THAT'S THE CANDLE LIT. NOW LET'S SEE IF—HEY, WHAT'S THAT YOU'VE FOUND?

THE LOOT FROM THAT BANK RAID! THAT SETTLES IT, THEN, CHARLIE—IT WAS LAFFERTY YOU SAW, ALL RIGHT!

LAFFERTY WON'T GIVE UP THAT MONEY SO EASILY! SURE AS A GUN'S A PISTOL HE'LL BE BACK FOR IT. YOU TAKE FIRST WATCH, CHARLIE, AND REMEMBER, IF HE COMES SNEAKING BACK DURING THE NIGHT, GRAB HIM!

Charlie settled down to wait, but it wasn't long before he got restless—and peckish! Luckily, Lafferty had laid in some provisions and amongst them was a whoppin' big jar o' honey. Charlie licked his lips as he reached for the jar . . .

Charlie just didn't spread the honey on a hunk of bread—he poured it on! But just as he opened his jaws to take a bite, a sudden CREAK broke the silence. Someone was squeezing through the boarded-up window!

Next moment, a shadowy figure slipped into the shack—just as young Danny had predicted! With an angry roar, Charlie hurled himself through the darkness.

One mighty clout from a hairy mitt knocked the intruder to the floor. Then quick as a flash, Charlie picked up the victim and thrust him into a cupboard.

The key was turned and away went Charlie, back to the office to get Danny out of his bed.

WHAT? HE'S COME BACK—AND YOU'VE CAUGHT HIM? GREAT! LET'S GO GET HIM!

Yep, young Danny was tickled pink—but not for long! For back at the shack, Charlie opened the cupboard and there, still dazed, sat not Luke Lafferty, but a big, brown bear! Charlie had made a mighty big mistake!

CRIKEY! THAT AIN'T LUKE, CHARLIE! AND YOU'VE MADE SUCH A RACKET IN HERE, HE AIN'T EVER GOING TO COME BACK NOW.

But Luke WAS coming back—at that very moment! For even as Charlie tried to explain away his mistake, the crook crept in and grabbed his loot!

YOU'VE SPOILED THE WHOLE SCHEME! WE MIGHT AS WELL PICK UP THE MONEY AND GO HOME!

Pick up the money? Not a chance! For when Danny and Charlie turned round, Luke and the loot had gone, and all that remained was a footprint in a sticky pool of honey.

Charlie saw the footprint, and the big bear smelt the honey—and that gave Charlie an idea!

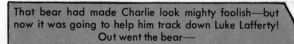

That bear had made Charlie look mighty foolish—but now it was going to help him track down Luke Lafferty! Out went the bear—

—then away it went on the honey trail.

ATTABOY, CHARLIE—IF LUKE LEFT THAT FOOTPRINT WE'LL SOON TRACK HIM DOWN!

Luke had left his horse with two of his henchmen while he stole back to the shack for the loot. Weighed down by the heavy bag, he got back just ahead of his pursuers.

QUICK, FELLAHS—PACK UP YOUR GEAR! THAT APE'S ON OUR TRAIL—WITH A BEAR!

A BEAR?

Luke and his pals might still have got away, if only the bear hadn't let out a roar at that moment. The three horses pricked up their ears and bolted.

UP THAT TREE—IT'S OUR ONLY CHANCE!

It was just too bad for Luke that he still had some trace of honey on his boot. That bear just loved honey . . .!

OH, MUVVER! IT'S SEEN US!

THAT'S THE STUFF! SHAKE THE VARMINTS DOWN!

When Charlie lent a hand, that tree really moved! It was like shaking apples out of a tree—only they were rotten apples!

Luke and his pals didn't raise any objections when Danny suggested they might care to carry all their loot back to the town. With an ape leading the way and a bear bringin' up the rear, they didn't dare argue!

For the first time in their crooked lives, these three mean hombres heaved a big sigh of relief when they were behind bars. At least they were safe from Charlie and his pal now!

As for that bear, well, Charlie reckoned he would be mighty handy to have around as a sort of bloodhound. But Danny was having none of it...

A BEAR AS WELL? NOTHIN' DOIN'! I GOT ENOUGH ON MY HANDS LOOKIN' AFTER YOU!

Charlie sure did feel sore at not bein' allowed to have a deputy bear all of his own, but the bear didn't mind a bit. With a jar of honey as a reward, it hurried out of town, leaving Danny and Charlie to their law-keepin' duties in Coyote Creek.

CHEER UP, CHARLIE! WITH YOU AROUND, COYOTE CREEK'S RUNNIN' OUT O' CROOKS SO FAST WE JUST DON'T NEED ANY MORE DEPUTIES!